The Other Side
Halloween Masque of Demons and Delusions

In this Halloween Masque, a young woman tainted by gossip is forced to flee to a House of Refuge but the dark cloisters are open to the invasion of demons and hallucinations.

Later, Victoria leaves the House of Refuge and travels far away to escape her tormentors but eventually she is driven by dark forces to the BigRiver that divides this world from the next.

At twilight, on a Halloween, she is visited by three masked devils that haunt the fleeing traveler on her great journey westward. They constantly torment Victoria and argue among themselves as to who is best to take her across the BigRiver.

The Lawyer tells the young woman that she will be safe with him.

Medicine T. Man offers her what he calls the elixir of life.

Preacher Boy identifies the drink as poison but it is too late for Victoria to avoid drinking it.

It is not clear if these visions are real or merely a dream at Halloween.

LIFE OF DREW CARSON

Sam Drew Carson was born in the North of Ireland and educated there at Wellington College and the Ulster Polytechnic. He completed his education in the USA at New Mexico Highlands University and the University of Arkansas and has traveled widely in North America, around the Atlantic and in Europe.

Drew worked as a seaman and fish-gutter in Vestmannaeyjar off the coast of Iceland. He lived and worked in the Irish and Western Isles Gaeltachts and was married in Welsh-speaking Carmarthen after which he honeymooned in Belfast. He has told his stories, composed and sung his songs, seeking storylines in Bristol and the English Westcountry. Drew has also lived and written in Nashville, Tennessee, in the wooded hills of Mid-America and from the Appalachians to the Ozarks. This was the culture that gave rise to the now worldwide Scotch-Irish country music.

In the USA, he also worked beside the bayous of the French-speaking Cajuns in the South and among the Western Spanish-speaking Navajos, Apaches and Pueblos of the Sangre de Cristo Mountains in New Mexico.

Drew has sailed far into the seas of old Gaelic and Oriental legend. After many years searching for inspiration for story and music, the author is still traveling and writing.

BOOKS BY THE SAME AUTHOR

ZENISUB
Fun and Games in Businezz
ISBN: 978-0-9561435-2-5

GOOD FOR A LAUGH
Six Funny Playscripts for Amateurs
ISBN: 978-0-9561435-3-2

HOME WITH A GOOD COMPANION
Amateur Pantomime Scripts for a Merry Winter
ISBN: 978-0-9561435-4-9

CLASSIC EUROPEAN LYRICS
Translated from the Gaelic, the French and Spanish
ISBN: 978-0-9561435-6-3

COMMONWEALTH
An Introduction to Business Economics
ISBN: 978-0-9561435-7-0

MISSING PERSONS
Detective Felix O'Neill in a Crime Adventure
ISBN: 978-0-9561435-8-7

WEREWOLF MURDERS
Detective Felix O'Neill in a Crime Adventure
ISBN: 978-0-9561435-9-4

ORIENTAL GOVERNESS
Detective Felix O'Neill in a Crime Adventure
ISBN: 978-1-908184-00-9

EASTER AND THE SPRINGTIME
Five Amateur Playscripts about New Life
ISBN: 978-1-908184-02-3

WALLWAVE THE YOUNG SEA WARRIOR
Adventures of War Queens and Battle Heroes
ISBN: 978-1-908184-03-0

WALLWAVE THE SEA PRINCE
Adventures of War Queens and Battle Heroes
ISBN: 978-1-908184-04-7

WALLWAVE THE SEA KING
Adventures of War Queens and Battle Heroes
ISBN: 978-1-908184-05-4

THAT SILVER SHORE
Easter Musical with Ten Songs
ISBN: 978-1-908184-06-1

THE OTHER SIDE
Halloween Masque of Demons and Delusions
ISBN: 978-1-908184-07-8

The Other Side

A HALLOWEEN MASQUE OF DEMONS AND DELUSIONS

DREW CARSON

Order from: https://www.createspace.com/4130580

Legals

Published by S. A. Carson,
29 Northleaze, Long Ashton, Bristol BS41 9HS, UK
Publisher's email: verygoodreading@googlemail.com

ISBN: 978-1-908184-07-8

CONTENTS

Page

ABOUT THE PLAY

This masque is a short symbolic play for at least seven male or female actors wearing masks representing the elemental types of:

1. witness of good and evil
2. eternity
3. mortality
4. lying and deceit.

THE PLAY CALLS FOR

Three Female Masks
(three sisters or three gossips)
Three Male Masks
(three devils or three demon suitors or three visitants)

MUSIC – 13 SONGS

Oh, my Mother, *p. 15*
Oh Holy Spirit may you Fall, *p.17*
Praise to the Great Creator, *p.17*
Oh, May the Holy Angels Watch, *p.25*
See you on the Other Side of BigRiver, *p.33*
A Land Further On, *p.37*
Mask of Death, *p.44*
The Hangman, *p.55*
Change Your Mind, *p.64*

CHARACTERS IN THE PLAY

Mother Refuge
– An Abbess in the House of Refuge
Prioress Shelter
– Assistant to Mother Refuge
Sister Harbor
– A prayerful sister in the House of Refuge

Victoria:
In Act One, she wears the mask of innocence.
In Acts Two and Three, she wears the white mask
of age, representing mortality. This mask is pale,
lean and bony and intense, framed by white hair.

Three Devils:
Zakir, Jeroz and Orav
In Acts Two and Three as
Knight, Shepherd, Sailor and
Preacher Boy, Lawyer, Medicine T. Man

Preacher Boy:
A lively dancing young man wearing the rainbow
mask of youth. This mask is smiling and brightly
colored, representing witness of good and evil.
The Lawyer:
A supernatural messenger wearing the gray mask
of maturity, representing eternity or the next
world. This mask shows a strong, lightly lined
oval face with gray hair surrounding.

Medicine T. Man:

A seller of medicine to cure all ills, wearing the black mask of death, representing a cheat. This mask is evil faced, dark with heavy lines, black eyes and hair.

PRODUCTION NOTES
Additional Dancers/Chorus:
Place: Anywhere in the great outback or remote country in any continent.
Time: Twilight
Season: Halloween
Four Masks: Four masks representing Youth, Maturity, Age and Death. Heavily stylized makeup should be used if masks are unavailable.
Stage Time: Will vary with treatment of verses - sung or chanted; approximately 1.1/2 hours.
Age Group: Audience and players of most ages, older children, teens, adults.
Set: One set with minor variations.

ACT ONE
THE TORMENTS BEGIN

SCENE ONE
DEMONIC PLOTS

There is a landscape where devils can walk from dream to dream among the world's sleepers. Eagerly they watch and wait for their next victim. Who will it be?

Enter the three devils *(Zakir, Jeroz and Orav) wearing the masks of Knight, Shepherd and Sailor. They are discussing their next victim.*

ZAKIR: We will confront the three malicious gossips and tell them stories of our supposed admiration for the young woman they call Victoria. Let us wear our masks of torment to encourage them to spread lies about her, for they are well-known in their town for stirring up trouble. We can give them plenty to gossip about.

The others eagerly rub their hands and nod in agreement.

Then let us masquerade and visit Victoria who is alone in her dreams now. We will set our traps of deceit for her.

JEROZ: Yes, we can also take the form of Lawyer, Medicine T. Man and Preacher. I can't wait to trap another victim and send them on their way towards BigRiver.

Orav is full of evil excitement as he joins in the plot and nods his approval.

ORAV: Yes, that will add to the number of people that we must drive to the point of destruction at the feast of Halloween – the time when humans fear the unseen forces that roam between sleeping and awaking.

The three devils whisper in each others ears as they scheme what to do next. Finally, they all rub their hands with invisible soap and look satisfied with their plans. They laugh, sneer and snigger.

All remain on stage as . . .

- Curtain -

SCENE TWO
THE HOUSE OF REFUGE

The House of Refuge is an old stone building. The action takes place in a high room with two arched windows that have balconies overlooking the sea. The walls are decorated with crosses. The room is furnished with bookshelves, a table or two and a couch. On each side of the couch there are tables with vases of red roses.

There are three throne-like chairs at which are seated the Abbess, Mother Refuge; her assistants, Prioress Shelter and Sister Harbor. Each wears a mask representing wisdom, piety, prayer or other religious symbolism. All are dressed in flowing black robes and each one wears a white sash with her name (Refuge, Harbor and Shelter) written across it. The robes display crosses and Christian religious symbols.

There are a few red roses scattered around the walls and furniture. No particular denomination is necessarily indicated.

A loud knock is heard coming from the door of the abbey. The door is opened by Prioress Shelter.

Enter Victoria, *a poor and naïve young woman who sells bread for a living. She is dressed in a simple, full-length dress and a long loose robe. She wears flat, walking or dancing shoes. Her hair is wrapped in a band with her name on it. Her mask represents an innocent young woman.*

PRIORESS SHELTER: Come in, my child.

Victoria is taken to the high room at the House of Refuge where she immediately begins to sing her song.

d   d   d s_1 m   m   m   d
O my Mother I have come from
d   m   s s   f m   r
Where the river slowly flows
r   m   f   f m   r m d
Where the banks of red, red roses
d   m   r s_1 t_1 r   d
Lead to gardens of the rose

Where the river meets the pathway
To the famous rosie bed
Where the banks of red, red roses
Lead to flowery roses red

There I seized the flowery blossoms
That I saw before my eyes
For the roses bloom forever
That I grasped with many sighs

For a moment the sisters stare at each other in confusion then Sister Harbor breaks the silence and speaks to the young woman.

SISTER HARBOR: My child, who are you? How can we help you?

VICTORIA *continues to sing*

THE OTHER SIDE

I'm Victoria, I have come here
I have traveled far and fleet
To find shelter and a harbor
In this abbey of retreat

I must flee way over seas now
Or I fear I will be dead
All my demon loves will kill me
For I plucked the roses red

ABBESS REFUGE *sings*
See the wide seas lie before you
We will hide you. Do not fear
I am Abbess Mother Refuge.
This is Prioress Shelter here
Here is also Sister Harbor
She will pray for you, my dear

Mother Refuge points to the scene of the seascape through the window. Then she sings once more

> m   m   m   f
> Seas of white foam:
> f_1 s_1 l_1 l_1 s_1 f_1
> Over all, over all.

d   d   d   d   d d l_1
Praise to the great Creator
d   d   d   d   d
Who made earth our home
d   d   r   m   r   d
And gave its wonder ways
d   d l_1 r   d   d taw_1
The bright and mighty heavens
taw_1 taw_1 s_1 d taw_1 taw_1 l_1
A hall for all the angels
m m m   f
Seas of white foam:
f_1 s_1 l_1 l_1 s_1 f_1
Over all, over all.

Sister Harbor welcomes Victoria. She smiles, takes her by the hand and sings

m s f m m r   r   d
O Holy Spirit may you fall
s_1 s_1 l_1 t_1 d m r
And all around inhabit
s   f   m r m m r d t_1 d
O Christ come soon upon us all
s_1 s_1 l_1 t_1 d m r d
And live with us in Spirit

From threats and sickness save us well
And heal us by your merit
Within our souls and bodies dwell
O hear us Holy Spirit.

From demons, from the vilest hell
From sins we all inherit
O Jesus may we be made whole
And holy by Your Spirit.

Sister Harbor continues to sing

d   d   d s$_1$ m   m   m   d
O please tell us how you come to
  d   m s   s f m r
Have to flee so far away
 r   m f   f   m r   m   d
Tell us how the demons found you
 d   m   r   s$_1$ t$_1$ r d
In your own home hideaway

d   d   d s m   m   m d
You were just a poor young maiden
d m   s s   f m   r
Toiling all the livelong day
 r   m f   f   m r   m   d
Tell us how the demons found you
 d   m   r   s   t r d
In your own home hideaway

All remain on stage as the sisters put their arms comfortingly around Victoria . . .

- Curtain -

The next scene contains dreamy, hazy flashbacks to the previous life of Victoria.

SCENE THREE
THE GOSSIPS

The scene is now set in the village square. A well stands in the center. It contains a bucket on a rope and a handle at the side for the raising and lowering of the bucket. In the background are village homes, trees, gardens and flowerbeds.

Enter from right the three demon suitors *dressed as medieval jesters. Each wears a demonic mask and displays a head banner or a sash as follows: Sailor, Knight and Shepherd.*

The three demons lurk and leer in the background, making as though to stab invisible victims to death. They slither and slide around and wave their arms and point threateningly at the audience but especially Victoria who is standing beside the village well.

Enter the three gossips *dressed in flowing robes and headdresses. They each carry a wicker basket. They wear three masks bearing the names: curiosity, rumor and malice.*

The gossips look in all directions, shading their eyes and scrutinizing everyone including the audience. They silently mime the appearance of talking in a gossipy manner as they nod to each other with open palms shielding their words.

All three gossips sing the first verse.

d d d s_1 m m m d	
See the damsel is most kindly	
d m s s f m r	
What a lovely lady she	
r m f f m r m d	
Yes, the young girl is so gracious	
d m r s_1 t_1 r d	
And a glorious lass is she	

See the damsel is most kindly
What a lovely lady she
Yes, the young girl is so gracious
And a glorious lass is she.

They look towards the lurking demons as they sing each of the following verses (same tune as p. 20). The demons don't respond but continue to lurk and leer in the background.

GOSSIP CURIOSITY:
Tell us, Sailor, you who live out
On the boats far off at sea
If your ship or sail or starlight
Is as beautiful as she.

GOSSIP RUMOR:
Tell us, Horseman, dressed in armor
On your horse, so gallantly
If your horse or law or armor
Is as beautiful as she.

GOSSIP MALICE:
Tell us, Shepherd, shepherd guarding
All the sheep you oversee
If your flock or glen or mountain
Is as beautiful as she.

THE OTHER SIDE

As Victoria sings, she looks confused and is waving her hand and pointing to each of the three gossips in turn.

---

d d   d s$_1$ m m m d
O my Mother I was lovely
d m   s s   f m   r
I was flower of the town
 r   m   f f   m   r m d
O my Mother then I went to
 d   m   r   s$_1$ t$_1$ r   d
Sell my bread all in the town

O my Mother they all told me
What a lovely girl in town
What a lovely girl is selling
Selling bread about the town

O my Mother when I went to
Sell my bread along the town
I was lovely O my Mother
I was flower of the town

All three gossips continue to whisper to each other as they look towards the lurking demons and to Victoria. Then they leave stage left.

The demons begin to sing to Victoria, using the same tune as before. They look at her with the expression of evil intent as they beckon to her with their arms outstretched.

THE SAILOR SINGS

> Come at dawning, well-beloved one
> Come at dawning of the day
> O my most desired beloved one
> Come at dawn, O come away

THE KNIGHT SINGS

> Most desired, with strongest feeling
> Come at light of dawn, I say.
> Come as day's still light is creeping
> Bring no friend with you, I pray

THE SHEPHERD SINGS

> Come as dawn's still light is seeping
> Bring no friend with you, I say
> Come as dawn's swift light is leaping
> Bring no close friend, come away.

Victoria is standing beside the well with a frightened expression on her face as she holds both her hands over her ears. She appears to be in torment as the flashbacks come to an end.

- Curtain -

SCENE FOUR
DEEP SLEEP

Back in the House of Refuge with the Abbess Mother Refuge, Prioress Shelter and Sister Harbor, Victoria addresses the three religious sisters.

She sings (to the same tune as before)

O my Mother I will die there
In the flowers I will be dead
In the garden of the blossoms
In the rose bed roses red

For I went to pluck the roses
But I found my loves instead
Now my loves my loves will kill me
Where I grasped the roses red

I have not one love but three loves
And they all would see me dead
They all wait for me and seek me
In the roses roses red

*Victoria walks sleepily back and forth
then sleeps on the couch surrounded by
roses.*

Prioress Shelter sings

```
d    r    m f m  s f-m    r
O may the holy angels watch
 s    m   d¹     t   l    s
Our rest and sleep this night
 r    m     f-f f m   l   l-law
O  Christ, Son of the living God
law  l   f   m    r    d
Do guard our beds with light
```

O High Prince of the Universe
Great Lord of Mystery
In sleep do show the Way of Truth
True visions let us see.

Let not the demons hurt nor harm
No terrifying dream
To rob us of our swift release
As we fall fast asleep.

And as You keep our sleeps and rests
From griefs and hindrance free
So let our waking and our works
Be white in holy peace.

The three religious sisters retire sleepily to another room, stage right, leaving Victoria alone.

Later in the evening as the lights dim to a twilight, the three demons enter and silently slither and stab around Victoria as though to kill her. She cries out in a low voice, moans and slumps back on the couch.

Looking back, as though reluctant to go, the three demons leave stage left with their masks still grinning.

- Curtain -

SCENE FIVE
THE FAREWELL

The same scene but it is now the next morning. Victoria remains on the couch where she has apparently been killed by the demons.

Mother Refuge and the two sisters enter stage and when they see Victoria lying limp on the couch they start to sing

```
    d   m - m   m - m   m – m - m   m   r - d
I'll  see you on the other side of BigRiver
    d   f - f   f       f – m - m   m   m - r
I'll see you where departed ones abide
    d   m   s - s   m   f - f   l   l - l
I'll see you sister and I'll see you, brother
    f   m - m   m - m   r - r   d
I'll see you on the other side.
```

```
   d    r    m    m    m    m    m    r    d    d
Where the deaf shall hear, where the lame shall leap
   d    d   f-f    f    f   m-m   m    r
Where the lonely shall be  lively  as  a  bride
   d    m        s    s    s      m     f-l   l    l
Where the eyes of the blind shall be opened for ever
   d    m    s   s-s   m      f      l   l-l
Where sorrow and dying will trouble us never
   d    m    s    s    s-m    f      l    l    l
We'll see you where the great waters heal us forever
   d    m    s    s   s-m     f    l   l-l
We'll see you on  the other side of the river
   f    m    m    m    r   r-r    d
We'll see you on the other side.
```

SISTER HARBOR: *(stares at the body of the young woman then gasps)* Mother Refuge, Victoria is not dead. Look, she is still breathing.

The sisters stare at her body for a moment then Mother Refuge gently touches her on the cheek and whispers in her ear.

MOTHER REFUGE: Victoria, my child.

Gradually the young woman appears to awaken from a deep sleep and looks around the room in confusion.

VICTORIA: Where am I? Who are you?

MOTHER REFUGE: You are safe here. This is the House of Refuge and I am Mother Refuge. This is Prioress Shelter and Sister Harbor.

Sister Harbor speaks up.

SISTER HARBOR: You came here last night and asked for our help.

PRIORESS SHELTER: Yes, you were in some kind of turmoil, my child. You said you were being tormented.

MOTHER REFUGE: Victoria you were tired so we let you sleep here.

VICTORIA: *(softly)* Thank you but I must get away from here soon. Can you help me?

PRIORESS SHELTER: Of course. We will get you anything you need - a horse and trap and some supplies.

MOTHER REFUGE: Please remember that you will always be welcome back here at any time. We will be praying for you.

VICTORIA: I don't understand what is happening to me. All I know is that I must get away and I must keep traveling.

Mother Refuge, Prioress Shelter and Sister Harbor all sing to the same tune as the last song (Where the deaf, etc).

Oh, we'll see you where departed ones are living forever
Where the long hills will blossom far and wide
Where everyone tends her own garden of trees
And the wine of the vine is long life and peace
Where the fish are flowing and frisky in the seas
And those who fish will be always at ease
We'll see you on the other side.

All four remain on stage in the same positions . . .

- Curtain -

ACT TWO
DEADLY VISITORS

SCENE ONE
A TIME TO REST

In the left background there is a wild country scene of rugged hills; mountains; trees turning gold; a winding, rushing river in the remote distance and a sky with the setting sun.

Right background is the nearer, broader banks of the river that winds across from the left background and a winding road runs from BigRiver to center stage.

Middle and foreground there are smaller trees, shrubs, rocks, bushes surrounding a wide space center stage, where painted scenery of a covered wagon or grazing horses may later be moved around and where the Chorus can sing the verses, engage in slow dancing and hand movements within the immediate framework and against the background of the remote hills and sky.

In the center there are the remains of an old campfire with some dying embers.

The scenery may be typical of any remote scenery where a wanderer might be expected to travel.

In this opening scene, center right, an old piebald horse is grazing. This may be painted scenery.

From time to time the sound of murmuring crickets can be heard, a wild dog or wolf howling in the background or night birds singing and chattering.

***Enter from left Victoria**, dressed as before. Due to the passage of time, she wears the white mask of age and carries some gear for her horse - an old rope, a bit, a bridle - and places it beside the grazing animal as though preparing to remount and ride on. An old shotgun lies among the other gear at the fire. She leans on the horse, pats it, talks to it and then sits down and dozes into a light sleep.*

*She is disturbed in sleep but not wakened by the **Chorus entering right** dressed in costumes similar to that of Victoria. They bow to her and raise their arms in salute and walk or dance around her as they softly sing –*

SEE YOU ON THE OTHER SIDE
OF BIGRIVER
Sung: Cheerfully and Sentimentally

VERSE ONE:

   d   r   m   m   m   m   m   r   d   d

Where the deaf shall hear, where the lame shall leap

   d   d   f-f   f   f   m-m   m   r

Where the lonely shall be lively as   a bride

   d   m   s   s   m   f-l   l   l

Where the eyes of the blind shall be opened for ever

   d   m   s   s-s   m   f   l   l-l

Where sorrow and dying will trouble us never

  d   m   s   s   s-m   f   l   l   l

I'll see you where the great waters heal us for ever

  d   m   s   s   s-m   f   l   l-l

I'll see you on the other side of the river

  f   m   m   m   r   r-r   d

I'll see you on the other side.

REFRAIN:

  d   m-m   m-m   m-m-m   m   r-d

I'll see you on the other side of BigRiver

  d   f-f   f   f-m-m   m-m   r

I'll see you when we cross the cruel tide

  d   m   s-s   m   f-f   l   l-l

I'll see you sister and I'll see you, brother

  f   m-m   m-m   r-r   d

I'll see you on the other side.

THE OTHER SIDE

REFRAIN:
I'll see you on the other side of BigRiver
I'll see you when we cross the cruel tide
I'll see you, sister and I'll see you brother
I'll see you on the other side.

VERSE ONE:
Where the deaf shall hear, where the lame shall leap
Where the lonely shall be lively as a bride
Where the eyes of the blind shall be opened for ever
Where sorrow and dying will trouble us never
I'll see you where the great waters heal us for ever
I'll see you on the other side of the river
I'll see you on the other side.

VERSE TWO:
O, I'll see you where departed ones are living forever
Where the long hills will blossom far and wide
Where everyone tends his own garden of trees
And the wine of the vine is long life and peace
Where the fish are flowing and frisky in the seas
And those who fish will be always at ease
I'll see you on the other side.

As the Chorus fade into the background they continue to softly sing as a lone wolf or wild dog howls.

VICTORIA: *(wakening up and talking to her horse)* We're going to have to keep going.

Victoria considers the matter as she talks to herself in a confused state of mind.

I think my days of traveling must be nearly over. So many years of wandering around just to find peace and rest from these demons that torment. I only want to live in peace and get on with my life and I seem to be losing track of time. It must be Halloween. I think the spirits are calling me away from this world but I'm not going to follow them over that BigRiver filled with evil spirits, dangerous currents and devil fish. I must get out of here in the morning and get on with my life – whatever is left of it.

      I'll not turn back. No, I'll just go away over to the other side. *(she points to the hills)* I'll get to those hills and avoid that great black river that seems to threaten.

She straightens up bravely but appears very confused as she looks around uneasily with a look of fear on her face. Then she rubs her head as if she is perspiring.

I must be all alone here. This strange uneasiness is just the spirits trying to call me to come over, this Halloween. Soon it will all pass at 12:00 tonight, I hope. I'll feel better then and I'll just be on my way.

There is the sound of wind as a wolf howls nearby. She shivers and looks around. The neigh of a horse is heard but it does not appear to be coming from Victoria's mount. She looks around startled and then walks up and down nervously.

(to the darkness, off stage) What was that? Who's out there? *(she goes to seize the old shotgun)* What's the use of a gun against spirits?

 The lights dim slightly.

She walks up and down, looks into the far hills to the left side of the BigRiver and sings . . .

A LAND FURTHER ON
Sung: Slow with Feeling

VERSE ONE:

s - s   l - s   m   d
Once I   was young

d - d   t₁   l - l₁   l₁
But now I am gray

l₁ - l₁   s₁   t₁ - r   l
I'm a lone traveler come

l   l - l   s   m d
To the end of my day

s   l - s   m   d
These times aren't as good

d - d   t₁   l₁ - l₁   l₁
As the good time now gone

l₁ - l₁   s₁   t₁ - r   l
So I'll take a long view

l   l - l   s - m   d
To a land further on

REFRAIN:

s   l - s   m - d   d - d   t₁   l₁ - l₁   l₁
I'm traveling along to a land further on

l₁   s₁ - t₁   r - l   s - d
I'm traveling away, away

VERSE ONE:
Once I was young
But now I am gray
I'm a lone traveler come
To the end of my day
These times aren't as good
As the good time now gone
So I'll take a long view
To a land further on

REFRAIN:
I'm traveling along to a land further on
I'm traveling away, away

VERSE TWO:
Through the outbacks and rocks
All the good singers come
Where the tin whistles weep
And the sad banjoes strum
I can hear up ahead
A sweet sorrowful song
For the great singers live
In that land further on

REFRAIN: *(again)*
I'm traveling along to a land further on
I'm traveling away, away

She looks again out over the hills to the left side of the river. BigRiver is in the distance right center background. With some satisfaction and nodding to herself, she beds down again and begins to doze off to sleep. She appears to be sleeping and then half-waking as one who is too nervous to sleep soundly. Desert noises, wild dogs, night creatures, a light wind rustles the leaves as crickets hiss. It is still twilight as . . .

- Curtain -

SCENE TWO
THE LAWMAN COMES

The same scene. It is still twilight and another white horse is standing beside Victoria's horse. It is strong and vigorous looking (painted scenery in most stage productions.)

A tall grayhaired Lawyer wearing a red shirt has just dismounted. He is in full riding and shooting gear with two large guns, fancy boots with spurs and a gunbelt across his chest. He is wearing a wide hat and scarf. His demeanor is military but with a slight hint of the swagger of a bandit chief. He wears the gray mask of maturity and approaches the young woman with a slow menacing walk. He is purposeful and intent, like one bearing an important message.

Victoria startles in her sleep as though troubled then wakes up, sees the Lawyer, rolls over and half-rises in fear. The creatures of the night still rustle and hiss as the Lawyer stalks over to Victoria.

VICTORIA: *(quickly and afraid)* Who are you? What do you want with me? *(noting* *his guns)* You're some kind of bandit, a fighting man . . an . . an . . outlaw, aren't you? I don't know you. I've never done you any harm. You just keep your distance *(she picks up the old shotgun, half heartedly)* or I'll shoot . . *(desperately)* well, I'm warning you.

The slow and deadly approach of the Lawyer contrasts with Victoria's haste and bumbling and fear. The Lawyer stops casually a short distance from her as a wild animal is heard screeching in the background.

LAWYER: Relax young woman, I'm not here to harm you. I'm just a lawman – a kind of security guard, a messenger from the other side of BigRiver. As a matter of fact these guns are for your protection, to make sure that you cross over safely. You'll be safe crossing over with me, Victoria. Just take it easy and get your belongings together now and we'll head on over . . .

VICTORIA: Now just a minute, Lawyer. You mean you want to take me into that

BigRiver - the black one with the deadly currents and the falls and the rocks? No thanks. I'd rather not go there, if you don't mind. No, that's not the way I'm going. *(fearfully)* No, you see it's like this. I'm going the other way over those hills. Yes, that's where I want to go - over those green hills. You thought I was going into the BigRiver. *(laughs weakly)* Why no, I'm not going in that direction. *(she stops laughing and starts trembling)*

LAWYER: Victoria, don't be afraid. I'm not here to take you into the black river. I'm here to help you cross over it safe and sound to the other side of BigRiver. There are friends of yours waiting for you on the other side of BigRiver. Everything is going to be pretty good, very soon.

VICTORIA: No thank you. I don't want to see those friends again.

LAWYER: *(smiling)* Really Victoria, no more old friends?

VICTORIA: Well, not now, not just yet . . maybe someday later . . . Yes, that's it, sometime later on when I feel more like meeting an old friend or two . . . See me some other time when I feel in a more friendly mood . . right now I don't feel too friendly. *(pulls herself up bravely)* Your sudden appearance has made me feel irritable and watchful and wary *(with sudden weakness)*. As a matter of fact I don't feel all that good, to tell you the truth *(sits down)*. But I still need to keep going in the other direction - over to those green hills there.

LAWYER: My friend, the way we travel in this life is beyond our control, after a certain point. So far we step and travel on our own but after that point the road is laid out for us. *(gently)* Forty is a good age to be - still young but strong and yet however hard anyone may try - no one can be forty forever *(in a friendly tone)*. And eighty is a good age to be - well aged, mature and wise but not too old. And yet, however hard any of us may try, no one can be eighty forever *(quietly and without menace)*. As a matter of fact, there comes an end to the road for even the best of men and women.

Lawyer sings THE MASK OF DEATH
Sung: Slowly and Melancholy

VERSE ONE:

l   fe   r   r m - fe   s - m   l
Youth wears a   many colored mask
  s   m   r - r   de   r
But underneath is gray
  l   r¹   r¹   t   r¹   de¹ - l   t
The streams of youth are rainbow bright
  s   m - m   fe   s - l
But swiftly swirl away
   l - l   r¹   t   r¹   de¹   l   t
Mature life wears a mask of gray
  s   m m - fe   s   l
But underneath is white
s - m   r   r   m   fe   s   m   l
For   in the bones, the worm crawls on,
  s   m   r   r   r   r
The clock strikes cold at night.

VERSE ONE:
Youth wears a many colored mask
But underneath is gray
The streams of youth are rainbow bright
But swiftly swirl away
Mature life wears a mask of gray
But underneath is white
For in the bones, the worm crawls on,
The clock strikes cold at night.

VERSE TWO:
Age wears a mask of wrinkled white
But underneath is black
The torture chamber groans and creaks
The screw, the claw, the wrack
Death wears a mask of earthen black
Destruction and decay
What lies beyond the mask of death
No living soul may say

REFRAIN:
The ages of a man step on
Step on from year to year
And faster the steps speed up
As end of life draws near.
Yes, ever faster steps speed up
Like breath that gasps for air
As man and woman run to flee
The dead hand of fear.

As the Lawyer finishes his song or recitation, he steps up to Victoria and beckons to her.

LAWYER: Come on, my dear lady.

VICTORIA: *(in fear)* No, not now, later . . Please, in a little while, I promise.

LAWYER: *(casually)* That's alright. In a little while. There's no hurry. I'll be back later. Remember, like I said, I only want to help you.

The Lawyer casually leaves stage right as Victoria anxiously watches him leave. At the same time the Lawyer's white horse fades into darkness as lights are deflected from it, indicating that the Lawyer rides off. Hoof beats are heard.

VICTORIA: *(she gasps in relief at the Lawyer's departure)* Phew . . that was a close call. I don't trust you, Mr. Lawyer. I'm not that much of a fool. I'm not in my dotage just yet. Older maybe, but I'm not a complete half-wit. Oh yes, come to protect me *(muttering to herself)* I've heard that one before.

Yes, from two thugs in the Old Town who said they wanted to protect me, then tried to rob me - ha, ha, didn't work then *(breathless)* and it won't work now *(defiantly)*. No, I'm not going with you, sir, now or later *(laughs hysterically then pauses and speaks thoughtfully)*. What does he want with me, anyway? I don't know him. Who is he? It must be a mistake. *(half relieved but trying to convince herself)* It must be a case of mistaken identity. Yes, that's it.

(pauses worried). Maybe it's a warning of death and destruction sometime in the future - that's not all bad - I can live with that. The future is a good time to die in - ha, ha *(she laughs hollowly)* everybody always wants to die in the future but not now - no not in the now.

Why, him and that white horse of his were just old ghosts trying to warn me of the future. But they've gone now and I'm not afraid. I'll not worry just now but I'll have to be careful with strangers like him turning up unexpectedly.

A horse is heard to whinny and a wild cat screeches and howls. Victoria is nervous at all the noises. She looks around fearfully and walks up and down edgily as . . .

- Curtain -

SCENE THREE
THE MAN OF MANY FACES

The same scene. Victoria has just awakened from sleep and yawns and stretches. The white horse has gone. The moon has replaced the sun. There is a more mellow light on stage. An old medicine wagon is now parked center. She is seen fussing around her campsite gathering together the gear and getting ready to move out.

VICTORIA: *(hearing footsteps)* No, not again. I'm not going with you, whoever you are. Who does that wagon belong to anyway? Who's out there?

Enter Preacher Boy from left*, holding a large book. He is young, active, moves around quickly with wide expansive gestures, speaks loudly and enunciates clearly like one used to addressing crowds. He wears the Rainbow Mask of Youth, a white tee shirt, a light suit and shining black shoes. He lopes around.*

PREACHER BOY: Not coming with me? Not going with Preacher Boy, eh? Well, that raises the important question. Where are you going - to a good place or a bad place?

VICTORIA: I'm going to a good place - the good green hills over there. *(she points to the left background)* Is that your wagon?

PREACHER BOY: That one, oh, no. That belongs to the evil one. Beware of it. But no, I mean on the other side of BigRiver. *(he lowers his voice tactfully)* In the next world where are you going? Let me ask you, sister . . .

His preaching is interrupted by the right stage **entrance of Medicine T. Man.** *He wears a dark suit, light collar and tie, white shoes and on his face the Black Mask of Death. He is straight and slow and dignified in his movements, in contrast to the loping around of Preacher Boy. He draws himself up straightly and points at arms length to Preacher Boy.*

MEDICINE T. MAN: You, Boy. Yes, you, you there! How dare you accost this respectable lady for money? *(spitting out the word)* Money - mere lucre.

Victoria ducks down between the two figures as though overwhelmed by their presence and looks up at them fearfully.

VICTORIA: Why are you all tormenting me like this? Go away. Leave me alone.

MEDICINE T. MAN: Yes ma'am. That's what this rogue is after - your money, good lady. I know him of old.
(in a stage whisper to Victoria) That's all any of these preachers are after - your money - to sell you deeds and rights to phony property in the next world. As if you were such a fool.
(turning to Preacher Boy) You lad, get out of here at once. *(Preacher Boy hesitates)* Or I'll *(slowly and threateningly)* deal-with-you-right-now.

PREACHER BOY: *(fearfully)* Now mister, I have a job to do . . .

MEDICINE T. MAN: *(sarcastically)* Yes - rob this woman. OUT, OUT. You filthy fraud. This second - GO.

Preacher Boy slinks low and lopes out fearfully leaving left stage.

MEDICINE T. MAN: *(to Victoria, in a solicitous tone of voice)* I'm sorry for the attempt on your finances. Obviously I arrived just in time and no more. I could see that young scoundrel eyeing my fine medicine wagon there - planning to steal it, no doubt. But forgive me, dear lady, a thousand apologies. Allow me to introduce myself. I arrived while you slept.
(aside: sinisterly) I often do that.
But out of consideration for you I did not awaken you.
(aside: menacingly) A regular habit of mine.
But you awoke anyhow and here you are - in need of my medicine.

VICTORIA: *(coolly)* What I need is to get rid of all you strange figures that have plagued me over the years, offering to take me over to the other side of BigRiver. All the medicine I need is to go the opposite way . . over there . . . (*she points*)

MEDICINE T. MAN: *(interrupting, gushingly)* Green hills, yes, but to do that you need health. I am T. Man, a Doctor of Medicine from the College of Eternal Healing but everyone calls me Medicine T. Man. Don't you realize, dear lady, that you are about to <u>die</u> DIE. Yes, death is about to visit you (*aside* - indeed is now doing so)

These strange figures that have visited you this Halloween are the delusions of a sick and dying human. Only I am real. See, touch me *(touches Victoria on the arm and leads her over to the medicine wagon)*

See, knock on wood, a real wagon. But where are those other shadowy figures . . out there lurking - delusions and devils masquerading, grimacing, shadowing, ready to spring back at you from the outer darkness *(slowly)* and lead you over the BigRiver of dreams and death. *(Draws back as though impressed with his own rhetoric)* But see, dear lady. I'm your friend, here to help.

VICTORIA: *(suspiciously)* How can you help me?

MEDICINE T. MAN: Well, I've driven out the others haven't I?

VICTORIA: Only the Preacher Boy.

MEDICINE T. MAN: Ah, but you didn't see me drive away the others - demons masquerading as humans while you were asleep. Anyhow you're in danger of . . *(craftily)* what do you think?

VICTORIA: *(tentatively)* Dying?

MEDICINE T. MAN: Right, dear lady. *(shakes head)* I'm afraid so but fortunately I have a medicine that will cure you of all ills. It doesn't cost much . . I'm in the business more from my great love of humanity. That's why brilliant men such as I become doctors - because we enjoy helping people - we get great satisfaction from healing people of all their troubles and ills *(sinisterly aside,* like "living", for instance) It makes me feel - somehow, I don't know how to describe it - happy inside - fulfilled, yes that's it - just to heal people, like you.

VICTORIA: No thanks I don't need it. I'm O.K. It's just Halloween with all those loose spirits around. I just want to get over these mountains and away from here and the BigRiver. I don't need any medicine, thank you.

MEDICINE T. MAN: But these strange spirits - the Lawyer out there waiting. Preacher Boy ready to spring back into action. And the worst of all . . out there.

VICTORIA: *(concerned and fearful)* Which one? Who . . . ?

MEDICINE T. MAN: Well, I'll tell you friend, because I know you need my medicine to save you. I'll just tell you.

VICTORIA: *(scared)* O.K. go ahead. I'm not afraid. Tell me.

MEDICINE T. MAN: *(evasively)* Well, I will then. But you promise not to fall apart with terror . . .

*Victoria nods, dumb with doubts and fear, then sits and crouches center stage.   Medicine T. Man sings **THE HANGMAN** while the **Chorus enters** left stage, dressed as before* and dance silently joining in the spoken or sung refrain, in a circle around Victoria and Medicine T. Man.   * or in dark robes*

THE HANGMAN
Sung: Slow and Sinister

VERSE ONE:

m   f   s   m - f - m   r - d   *m* r - r
Well, I bid goodbye to Lazarus

m - f *s* - m   f   m   r   d l_1
BigRiver's tide runs fierce and black

m   f   *s*   m   f   m   r   d *m* r   r
For the cunning hangman is a-standing by

s_1 l_1 d - d   m r d l_1 s_1
With the poison behind his back

m   f   s   m   f - m - r   d   m   r - r
For he is a bakersman of moldy bread

m - f   s   m   f   m   r - d l_1
Who fills up many a hungry tomb

m - f   s   m f m   r   d   m   r - r
A   vile confectioner of bulging eyes

s_1 - l_1 d   m   r   r - d l_1 s_1
Who doles out the syrup of doom

THE OTHER SIDE

REFRAIN:

m - f s   m f   m   r   d - m   r   r

O, how can one man read another man's soul

  m   f   s   s - s   m f - m   r   d l_1

When he tries to judge the wrong from the right?

m - f s - m m f m r d   m r   r

For   only   a   terrible traveler sails

  s_1 l_1 d   m r - d l_1 s_1

Through the swift BigRiver of Night.

VERSE ONE:

Well, I bid goodbye to Lazarus
BigRiver's tide runs fierce and black
For the cunning hangman is a-standing by
With the poison behind his back
For he is a bakersman of moldy bread
Who fills up many a hungry tomb
A vile confectioner of bulging eyes
Who doles out the syrup of doom

REFRAIN:

VERSE TWO:

Now, the hangman tends his trees with hateful glee
He waters the dying gallows tree
He prunes it primly to cut off dead fruit
He attends it lovingly
He raises up his deadly plants
Yes he raises them up so high on high
Like some strange gardener who screams with joy
Just to see his dread flowers die

REFRAIN:

VERSE THREE:
O the cunning hangman hides and weeps as he
Throws the flowers far from the shores of life
Though the hangman's eye is soft, his hand is hard
And his heart is as cold as a knife
And yet all must one day pass along this way
To a cold and wild and foreign shore
Even the grim hangman will one day fall
Into that Great Trapdoor

Chorus leave *slowly, right stage as Victoria looks around confused and openly afraid.*

VICTORIA: Can you give me some protection from this hangman . . this killer?

MEDICINE T. MAN: You see Victoria, the Hangman is Death.
(*turns to audience in an aside, unheard by Victoria* – I am also the Hangman).
You're going to die unless you drink my medicine. That's the sad truth. See, here, I have a bottle on me. Take a drink. It'll not cost you much.
(*aside* - just everything you have)

Just a dollar dear lady and great protection from all death and disease.

He hands Victoria a small bottle of liquid. She accepts the bottle, looking around fearfully.

VICTORIA: *(gratefully)* Thank you Mr. Medicine Man. I'll not forget this favor.

MEDICINE T. MAN: *(aside, with menace and sneering spite* - No, you won't have time to).

Victoria drinks the contents of the bottle. Suddenly she clutches her stomach in pain and then crouches down in agony. The medicine man's manner changes from his former gentlemanly, urbane way to his alternative sneering snide aside personality.

VICTORIA: What was this? What was in that bottle, Mr. Medicine Man?

MEDICINE T. MAN: *(loudly and defiantly)* Poison. Death.

VICTORIA: No, No. You fooled me. Why? Please, please you're a medicine man. Give me the cure. You must have the antidote.

MEDICINE T. MAN: There's no cure for death. You'll die soon. Without that bottle you might have lived another 10 or 20 years. *(laughs)* Now you are as good as dead.

VICTORIA: Give me the cure, I beg you *(she weeps)* Heal me, Medicine Man.

MEDICINE T. MAN: Me cure you? Ha, Ha. Don't be stupid. I couldn't heal you even if I wanted to but I don't care to anyway.

VICTORIA: Liar, cheat. I'll kill you.

MEDICINE T. MAN: *(leaving)* You'll kill me - that's rich.

Medicine T. Man begins to dance around grotesquely, mocking Victoria and aping a prize fighter.

MEDICINE T. MAN: Oh yes, dear lady, let's see you try it - come on *(thumbs his nose and paws the air in fake pugilism)* come on now - fair fight, Marquis of Queensbury Rules - put one here. *(clenches his fists and points to his chin. He dances around aggressively. Victoria is calmer but stunned)*

Don't you realize who I really am? I am Death - the man of many faces. My middle name is time - that's what the T stands for - Time. And Time has just caught up with you. Your time is up. Ha, Ha *(he laughs)* You're going to die very soon. You fool. And to think that you let me drive out silly, harmless Preacher Boy. *(he laughs loudly and sinisterly as he leaves the stage right)*

The lights dim a little more and light is deflected from the medicine wagon as he leaves (or he may drive it away, if feasible). The sound of his wagon, horse, bells, jingling harness, horses' hooves and his laughter echo after him.

Victoria is devastated and in some pain, though not quite dying yet. She is sad and somber, more thoughtful and resigned to her fate, less fearful than before, perhaps just a little apprehensive. But it is all too late and death is too close for a massive fear of the unknown.

VICTORIA: Now I understand things a little better *(in a somber and nostalgic mood)*. It seems like only a few weeks ago that I was a happy young woman, so full of life and fun but time has won. I remember now, my life started to fall apart when those gossips began tormenting me with their stories of mysterious admirers and spreading malicious rumors about me. *(solemnly)* Time is the winner now. Yes, it's difficult to get the better of time.

(sadly and calmly) Time is the dreary detective who dogs our footsteps and destroys our peace of mind. Time is the runner who cheats in the race and despite his cheating - wins. We lose the race and are amazed. We cannot believe that we have lost. But how Time cheats and deceives us! Time - if you listen closely to his footsteps, ticks away slowly, in seconds. Craftily and cunningly he pretends to go slowly.

But if you take your attention away from Time's slow steps, to look at your work or leisure, Time jumps up and becomes another person and cheats you. He flies above you or runs unexpectedly across fields or takes short cuts when your back is turned even for a moment. He leaps over ravines, vaults over creeks and trees and robs you in every way to get there before you could possibly expect it. Then the race is over before you know it. You have lost and Time has won. Time is the cheat and Cheat is now the winner.

Victoria stretches wide her arms and faces towards the moon, then she slowly brings her hands down on her head in a gesture of despair. She drops both her arms limply by her sides and bows her head as one who has been defeated by fate . . .

- Curtain -

SCENE FOUR
MAKE OR BREAK

The same scene. The medicine wagon has gone. Victoria is sick and coughs while cleaning up her camp, getting together her possessions and preparing to move out. Yellow pale light of the moon is now shining a little more brightly than before. The night sounds, such as birds, breeze in the trees, insects continue but at a more subdued level for the present. She swats away a fly and fusses at her horse.

VICTORIA: *(to her horse)* Come on old friend, settle down. We're getting out of here right now, traveling to a good country far away from BigRiver.

Enter Preacher Boy *dressed and masked as before, still carrying the same large book which he later places on a tree trunk or stone, after he continues his prancing and dancing all around stage.*

Victoria looks shocked to see him back again.

PREACHER BOY: Hello again. You look very despondent. What's your problem? Anyway, don't answer me yet. Just listen to what I have to say first and then you can give me your answer.

He sings

CHANGE YOUR MIND.
Sung: Slow and Pleading

VERSE ONE:
f s   l - l   f   d   taw₁ l₁
Still, do you doubt the teaching
taw₁ d   f   f - f   f
Of those who gladly tell?
  s l   s   l   taw d¹ d¹   l d¹
Maybe your prayers have not been answered,
taw   r   m   r   d
Life not gone so well?
  l d¹ l   d¹ - d¹   taw - taw   l
Or do you doubt the songs of hope
   l   f - f   r - r   taw
That ring from many a bell?
f s   l - l   f   d   taw₁
Then pray to find the way
  l₁   taw₁ d f
Change your mind.

THE OTHER SIDE

VERSE ONE:
Still, do you doubt the teaching
of those who gladly tell?
Maybe your prayers have not been answered,
life not gone so well?
Or do you doubt the songs of hope
that ring from many a bell?
Then pray to find the way
Change your mind.

VERSE TWO:
O can you find no peace
after searching high and low?
Do you believe that this short life
is all that we can know?
That after we have died
there is no place else to go?
O pray to find the way
Change your mind.

VERSE THREE:
Do you believe there is no heaven,
no eternal plan?
Do you not see in nature
the work of one great hand?
Don't you know that all the sorrow
in this world is made by man?
Think it over one more time
And pray to find the way
Change your mind.

VICTORIA: *(looking coolly at the Preacher Boy's prancing).* O.K. Preacher Boy. *(with a hint of disappointment, sighing)* You're too late. You might as well get out of here while you can before the masqueraders return. What am I saying? You could be one of them trying to torment me? I don't really know who you are. Are you a demon or an angel? I don't understand you.

PREACHER BOY: Why not? What harm did I do? I tried to warn you but you wouldn't listen. Remember, I told you to watch out for that Medicine Man. But you simply wouldn't listen.

VICTORIA: *(relenting just a little)* Well, maybe so. But you ran off. You let me down when I needed you most.

PREACHER BOY: No. No. You can't blame me. All men fear the Medicine Man. I am only a Witness to Truth, but I'm still human enough *(looking around fearfully)* to fear the man of many names. *(He recites the names slowly and sinisterly)* The Hangman, Old Father Time, The Grim

Reaper, The Medicine Man, The Cheat, The Fake. Though I call him <u>Break</u> - I think that's his best name.

VICTORIA: *(puzzled and coughing badly)* Break? Break? I don't understand. That's not a real name. What are you trying to say to me?

PREACHER BOY: *(holding out both his hands to Victoria - palm held up towards Victoria)* Look. What's written on my right palm? See?

VICTORIA: *(approaching intrigued and squinting closely at Preacher Boy's right palm)* MAKE - <u>Make.</u>

PREACHER BOY: *(nodding and looking pleased, as though establishing a point)* Hmm. *(brightly)* And what's written on my left palm?

VICTORIA: *(as before, peering at upheld palm)* B.R.E.A.K. Break. Right?

PREACHER BOY: *(as one who has scored a great point. Overjoyed).* Right! Very good! And these two choices will <u>Make</u> or <u>Break</u> you.

Every word that you speak, every thought that you think, every deed that you do – flies out to the far wall of the universe where it is multiplied ten-fold for either good or ill and then bounces back to you in person so that you enjoy the effect of your own words or thoughts or deeds multiplied by ten. What you send out becomes a part of your life ten times over. So be careful what you send.

VICTORIA: *(puzzled again)* What are you trying to tell me?

PREACHER BOY: Understanding the difference between these two hands will help you over BigRiver.

VICTORIA: I'm not going there friend, get that idea out of your head. *(coughs)*

PREACHER BOY: *(brightly, as one offering a last chance)* It's not too late to take "MAKE" the right hand of help. It's too late to avoid BREAK - the Medicine Man. But here, take this hand *(dropping his left hand to his side and holding up the right palm turning it into a proffered handshake posture)* - now take "MAKE".

VICTORIA: *(drawing back suspiciously and putting her right hand protectively behind her back)*. I don't understand what this is all about. What exactly does it mean MAKE or BREAK?

PREACHER BOY: *(dancing around for joy)* You really want to know? Great, that's what I'm here for - to gladly tell. You're a great lady. Let me tell you the story of MAKE or BREAK. You've heard the old saying - It'll either "make or break you," right?

Preacher Boy stops dancing and crouches down eagerly as he tells his story to the weary traveler.

VICTORIA: Uh, Huh, *(nods)*

PREACHER BOY: Well. Those are the two opposites - see, make or break. Medicine T. Man - old Break or me a young witness to Make - *(holds up his right palm)*.

Yes, Make . . or *(holds up his left palm)* Break. That's what the world is all about and all the people in it belong to just Two Parties. There are only two kinds of men and women, those who make and those who break. There's no neutral, because if you do nothing, you help the biggest party and that is Break. By doing nothing, you give the breaks a chance to smash up, to break things and people. But, though most folk belong to the Break Party, the few who belong to the Make Party will surely win in the end. Break causes robbery, war and lies and murder and violence. Break people spend their lives . . .

VICTORIA: Grabbing.

PREACHER BOY: Well, I suppose that greed is behind it all and trying to gain more power or get more wealth for themselves but really, if that's all they did, life would be just fine. No - what Break people really want most is to tear down what the Make people do and sabotage and destroy the Make people and drive them into the jungle and into the grave, so they only grab to deprive others.

Now Make people *(Preacher Boy holds his right hand and flexes his fingers)* try to build up and create new things - cities, houses, books, knowledge of truth, See? Make is the builder, the friend, the honest craftsman - he likes to see people do well.

Break *(Preacher Boy clenches his left fist and shakes it)* is the destroyer, the enemy, the tearer down. He would rather see <u>himself</u> destroyed than see anyone else succeed. Yes he would kill himself even to destroy a <u>small part</u> of you.

VICTORIA: That's a bad enemy to have. *(looks around in fear).*

PREACHER BOY: Yes, remember, even Break admitted that he must also one day go into the great trapdoor. It didn't seem to faze him any. All he cares about is death anyway. Now, not only is the world divided between Make or Break - that would be bad enough, but it's worse than that. The whole universe is also so divided, see! All the great spiritual forces of the universe are forms of either Make or Break. Now, my friend, which of my hands will you grasp? The left hand of Break or the right hand of Make? *(he holds out both his hands as for a handshake)* Which is it?

VICTORIA: *(impressed with Preacher Boy's story and somewhat pleased to understand it)* Why, Preacher Boy, I hold you no ill will, exactly. I'll take your right hand - "Make" *(she shakes hands warmly with Preacher Boy who is overjoyed, dances about, seizes up his book again and begins to wave it like a flag).*

PREACHER BOY: Hear more from the Book of Knowledge . . all music, all songs, all writing is either Make or Break, see . . .

VICTORIA: *(shaking her head, but still pleased with Preacher Boy)* I don't need any more knowledge than what you have just told me. It's too late for me now, I'm afraid. Some of Break's old Medicine Man's friends seem to be lurking around here. I need to get going well away from BigRiver and all these strange apparitions.

PREACHER BOY: Now, it's too late to avoid BigRiver but it's never too late for understanding . . .

VICTORIA: *(listening)* Shush . . . There's something coming.

Preacher Boy listens and nods shakily.

PREACHER BOY: *(fearful)* I think you're right. I've preached long enough. It's time for me to find others who need to hear my story. Take my right hand one more time. *(they shake hands)* Remember Make is the true hand, not Break, Old Friend. Make not Break.

He leaves stage left, still dancing around but more afraid and in a hurry.

VICTORIA: *(waving goodbye)* Thanks for your story Preacher Boy – I think.

Victoria remains on stage waving goodbye to Preacher Boy, off stage left. Then she turns with some curiosity and some apprehension to see who is approaching, also off stage, right. She lifts up her old shotgun and peers into the darkness as the night noises begin to rise up more loudly - Cats, wild dogs or wolves are heard loudly in the distance. A sudden stillness, a near silence, descends as only the insects and breezes are heard for a few moments of expectation. Victoria remains pointing gun to off stage right.

VICTORIA: Who's there? I'm warning you. Stay away . . .

- Curtain -

ACT THREE
THE LONE TWILIGHT ROAD

SCENE ONE
THE FAR CAMPFIRES

The same scene later in the night. The moon is less bright and the stage is dimly lit. There are some dim lights as of campfires along the road in the direction of BigRiver. Victoria's horse has moved some way along the road to BigRiver, right stage. If stage space is limited, her horse may be off stage.

VICTORIA: Come back here old friend. But no, I'll follow after you instead for a little way. It's now time for us to leave this place. *(she moves a little way mid right stage along the road to BigRiver).*

***Enter** Medicine T. Man right stage.*

VICTORIA: Oh no, not you again. What do you want with me? Why don't you leave me in peace.

MEDICINE T. MAN: I hear you've been listening to that Preacher Boy. I hope you didn't give him any of your money.

VICTORIA: You asked me that before. But he has never tried to get any money from me. Why do you always suspect that he's a scrounger?

MEDICINE T. MAN: Because he lives on other people's money, that's why. He doesn't need to ask you for it directly. Most people give to him lavishly because he makes them so happy with his MAKE or BREAK line of entertainment.

VICTORIA: I have never given him a penny. So forget it.

MEDICINE T. MAN: I suppose he's told you all about MAKE or BREAK. *(he holds up his hands palm forward like Preacher Boy)* Oh yes, make or break. One part of his story is true. He says he is MAKE and he is certainly on the make, that's how he wheedles away most people's money. Oh yes, he is on the make alright. It's clear that you've never come across any of these preacher boys before.

He holds a bottle of some strong liquid. Laughing, he holds it out tauntingly to Victoria.

MEDICINE T. MAN: Victoria, how about another drink? *(laughs)* Just one for the road. I see you're headed out to BigRiver, Ha, Ha.

Medicine T. Man sings the refrain of **THE HANGMAN** *as he slowly retreats to stage left.*

REFRAIN:
O, how can one man read another man's soul
When he tries to judge the wrong from the right?
For only a terrible traveler sails
Through the swift BigRiver of Night?

Enter *Preacher Boy, left.*

VICTORIA: Oh no, am I never going to get peace from these tormentors.

PREACHER BOY: *(holding his book again, he places it nearby then holds out his two hands towards Victoria - palm forward as before).* Remember "Make" or "Break". You've chosen the good one.

*Before Victoria gets a chance to speak to him, Preacher Boy sings the second verse of **CHANGE YOUR MIND.***

O can you find no peace
after searching high and low?
Do you believe that this short life
is all that we can know?
That after we have died
there is no place else to go?
O pray to find the truth
Change your mind.

Then he suddenly retreats to stage left, alongside Medicine T. Man and waves his right hand at Victoria as she is about to turn her back and proceed along the road towards BigRiver.

*From the right, **enter** the Grey Masked Lawyer. He strides around the center stage. But before he joins Medicine T.*

Man and Preacher Boy at left, he speaks to Victoria.

LAWYER: There comes a time for all mortals to go down that lone twilight road to BigRiver. I'll come with you a little way for company.

*He sings refrain of **THE MASK OF DEATH**.*

The ages of a man step on
Step on from year to year
And faster the steps speed up
As end of life draws near.
Yes, even faster steps speed up
Like breath that gasps for air
As man and woman run to flee
The dead hand of fear

VICTORIA: No thanks. I don't want any of you for company. I want to go on alone.

LAWYER: If you need a little company part of the way, just give me a shout.

VICTORIA: I need to travel on alone. *(to all three masked figures)* Perhaps you three are not real. Perhaps it's all a dream and you're all only delusions. *(the others draw back from her as though wounded)* Maybe you've all come to give me understanding - to clear my mind as to where I'm going - to give me a clear view through the last window on life.

Are you real creatures or ghosts of Halloween or maybe this is my troubled deathday? I wish I knew for sure exactly what's been happening to me.

Suddenly the three demons start to squirm and hiss at Victoria.

All I know is that I must go on. I see bright campfires up ahead there like the ones I saw when I was a young child. They will be my guide – not you.

She moves a little further towards the BigRiver right, then turns to face the audience, also looking left stage to the three masked figures. They begin to threaten Victoria, but are held back as by an invisible force.
All three, Medicine T. Man, Preacher Boy and the Lawyer show their true

menace and ill-will towards Victoria as she now becomes a lone and isolated figure.

Medicine T. Man holds up high the bottle of poison, as before, but now he is more serious - less joking, less taunting and jocular. There is a sinister air about his gestures and like the others he is now viciously threatening.

Preacher Boy waves the left hand of "Break" at Victoria, clenching and unclenching his fist. He seizes up his Book of Wisdom, waves it around and throws it at Victoria.

Then Lawyer appears to be upset at Victoria's refusal to accept his offer of help and guidance. He draws first one and then his other gun, takes cold-blooded aim at Victoria, shoots twice at her silently, misses both shots. She ducks slightly at each shot, as though they passed over her head, but is otherwise unperturbed.

This sea-change in their attitude springs from Victoria's speech "perhaps you are all delusions" leaving the audience with the unanswered question "are they real or merely ghosts of Halloween - even subjective creatures?"

However, they appear to be bound by a force beyond their control, and seem to face an invisible pane of glass between themselves and Victoria. They begin to claw and hammer at the unseen barrier. They all grimace horribly. They now represent the throes of death of Victoria.

***Enter** the Choir of Dancers as before and remain right stage facing the three masked demons.*

The Medicine T. Man again waves the poison bottle at Victoria.

Preacher Boy shakes his left fist and hides his right hand behind his back.

The Lawyer again takes aim, slowly and carefully but again appears to miss.

*Victoria sings or chants on her own the four verses of **A LAND FURTHER ON**.*

THE OTHER SIDE

The dancers join in the refrain after each verse. The Dancers may also give light choral backing to each of the verses as she sings solo or with very light vocal backing:

VERSE ONE:
Once I was young
But now I am gray
I'm a lone traveler come
To the end of my day
These times aren't as good
As the good times now gone
So I'll take a long view
To a land further on

REFRAIN:
Dancers join backing for song's refrain.
I'm traveling along to a land further on
I'm traveling away, away

VERSE TWO:
Through outback and rocks
All the good singers come
Where the tin whistles weep
And the sad banjos strum
I can hear up ahead
A sweet sorrowful song
For the great singer's live
In that land further on

The lights dim a little, highlighting the campfires in the distance as Victoria moves a little further towards BigRiver.

The three masked figures left stage, kneel on one knee and point towards her as they repeat the refrain following Verses 3 and 4.

The dancers move slowly and solemnly left and center stage, sometimes pointing at the three masked figures left. Sometimes they face Victoria, and heartbrokenly bow their heads towards her as they occasionally give her some choral backing, either singing or if a recitation is used, chanting "aaah no" and clapping their hands. The dancers should suggest a sad parting, a misfortune even a tragedy, a time of regret, with pointing, sighing, clapping hands or bowing of heads.

Victoria sings Verse 3 solo.

VERSE THREE:
There's an old scout up there
With his hair white as snow
Where the calm creeks and springs
Are contented and slow
I'll look for his campfires
To guide me along
That lone twilight road
To a land further on

REFRAIN:
I'm traveling along to a land further on
I'm traveling away, away

As before, joined in by dancers, the three masked figures, left stage, join in the Refrain in the second person.

You're traveling along to a land further on
You're traveling away, away.

Victoria sings Verse 4 solo.

VERSE FOUR:
Though some songs I'll sing
Will be old songs and cold
As I dream of the days
When I walked tall and bold
Yet I'll sing of the new drives
From sunset to dawn
To a green hill ahead
To a land further on

REFRAIN:

As before, joined in by dancers, the three masked figures, left stage, join in the Refrain in the second person.

You're traveling along to a land further on
You're traveling away, away.

The three masked figures at left stage stand quietly in unison as they cease their menacing gestures and remain fairly still.

You are on your own now, Victoria, completely on your own.

She goes a little further towards the BigRiver, as light fades and the voices of the singers finish the refrain.

REFRAIN:

We're all traveling on to a land further on
We're traveling a long, long way.

Voices fade as Victoria becomes lost left center in the hills and woods and bushes that line the path to BigRiver. She is seen to disappear either by moving into the scenery or by fading lights. She does not reappear until the curtain calls and does not appear in the final scene.

- Curtain -

SCENE TWO
FINALE - THE ROAD TO BIGRIVER

This final scene is a continuation of the previous scene and is simply a finale, in the form of a last salute to Victoria.

The three masked demons - Medicine T. Man, Lawyer and Preacher Boy are gradually highlighted again as the lights are brightened slowly. They all remain left stage, in similar kneeling positions to their previous posture. They are joined by the three gossips and the sisters from the House of Refuge. They all point towards the BigRiver, to approximately where Victoria disappeared on the trail, right center stage.

The dancers, dressed as before, settle down to their knees, center and right stage. They are also pointing to where Victoria disappeared in the previous *scene. They all sing **SEE YOU ON THE OTHER SIDE OF BIG RIVER** - all verses, including the Refrain*

REFRAIN:
I'll see you on the other side of BigRiver
I'll see you when we cross the cruel tide
I'll see you, sister, and I'll see you, brother
I'll see you on the other side

VERSE ONE:
Where the deaf shall hear, where the lame shall leap
Where the lonely shall be lively as a bride
Where the eyes of the blind shall be opened forever
Where sorrow and dying will trouble us never
I'll see where the great waters heals us for ever
I'll see you on the other side of the river
I'll see you on the other side.

VERSE TWO:
O I'll see you where departed ones are living forever
Where the long hills will blossom far and wide
Where everyone tends his own garden of trees
And the wine of the vine is long life and peace
Where the fish are flowing and frisky in the seas
And those who fish will be always at ease
I'll see you on the other side.

Slowly all the members of the cast come on stage. They turn away from the

BigRiver and point to the audience. They repeat the chorus as they continue to point at the audience.

We're all traveling on to a land further on
We're traveling a long, long way.

- Curtain -

Note on curtain calls:
Mother Refuge
Prioress Shelter
Sister Harbor
The Three Gossips
The Three Demons
Victoria

The final movie credits may include cameo shots of all the actors removing their masks - an old idea that might well be revived. Similarly, in stage curtain calls - the actors should remove their masks.

- Curtain –

END OF PLAYSCRIPT

APPENDIX
FIVE FINGER EXERCISE
Simple Instructions on
How to Play the Tunes

Music is presented in the form of tonic sol-fa. Tonic sol-fa is the written form of music for both beginners and virtuosos – those who do not need guidance on timing, arrangements or chords – those who need only the basic tune.

1. Hitting the Right Note
2. White Keys - Stick-On Labels
3. Black Keys - Stick-On Labels
4. Getting the Timing Right
5. Summary

HITTING THE RIGHT NOTE

C is the white note just to the left of the two black notes side by side. Find Middle C on your keyboard. A register is the level of a set of tonic sol-fa. Here is the location of Middle C on a standard three register keyboard. The white note in the exact middle of any keyboard is Middle C (in staff) and Doh (in tonic sol-fa).

The tunes in this songbook can all be played on these three middle registers. Larger keyboards may have additional higher or lower registers but these will not be needed for the simple basic tunes in this book.

C is always Doh and going up from Middle C is the central set of tonic sol-fa:

Doh, Ray, Me, Fah, Soh, Lah, Te.

The next note is also a C and is the Doh higher than Central Doh. This starts off the next register of tonic sol-fa notes.

The Middle Set of tonic sol-fa have no subscript or superscript: d, r, m, f, s, l, t.

The Lower Register (set of tonic sol-fa) have subscripts as follows: d_1, r_1, m_1, f_1, s_1, l_1, t_1.

The Higher Register (set of tonic sol-fa) have superscripts as follows: d^1, r^1, m^1, f^1, s^1, l^1, t^1.
Here is a complete set of labels, for the white and black keys, to stick onto your central basic keyboard.

WHITE KEYS: STICK-ON LABELS FOR YOUR KEYBOARD

LOWER REGISTER	Doh_1	Ray_1	Me_1	Fah_1	Soh_1	Lah_1	Te_1
MIDDLE REGISTER	Doh	Ray	Me	Fah	Soh	Lah	Te
HIGHER REGISTER	Doh^1	Ray^1	Me^1	Fah^1	Soh^1	Lah^1	Te^1

WHITE STICK-ON NOTE INSTRUCTIONS

These are to be stuck on to your keyboard to show you which notes to play as you follow the Tonic Sol-fa music set out in each song.
1. The seven white notes with subscripts (lower register) lead up to Middle C.

2. Middle C starts off the middle register of seven white notes that have neither subscripts nor superscript.
3. The seven white notes with superscripts (higher register) follows on after the middle register.

Only the last three white notes of the lower register and the first white note of the higher register are shown with the middle register in the keyboard diagram.

THE BLACK KEYS

The black keys in each register are as follows:
de, maw, fe, law, taw.

The five black keys in the lower register
have subscripts
The five black keys in the middle register
have no subscripts or superscripts
The five black keys in the higher register
have superscripts.

Here are the three sets of labels to stick onto the black notes on your keyboard.

LOWER REGISTER	De_1	Maw_1	Fe_1	Law_1	Taw_1
MIDDLE REGISTER	De	Maw	Fe	Law	Taw
HIGHER REGISTER	De^1	Maw^1	Fe^1	Law^1	Taw^1

GETTING THE TIMING RIGHT

(1)   Notes that are grouped together have hyphens between them - to show that they are played together. (eg: d - f - l). This does not mean that such notes are speeded up, only that they are joined together.

(2)   Notes that are to be held longer than average are written in italics - that is to say they are sloped to the right (eg: *d* or *s*).

(3)   Try to follow the hints at the head of each tune (eg: slow and simple or fast and warlike).Keep a steady and regular beat whether the tune is fast or slow (eg: tap your foot or get a friend to tap out an even measured beat).

SUMMARY

Below is a diagram of all three registers - Lower, Middle and Higher. Of course, on many keyboards and pianos there are more than these three registers but these keys are all that you will need to play the simple tunes in this songbook

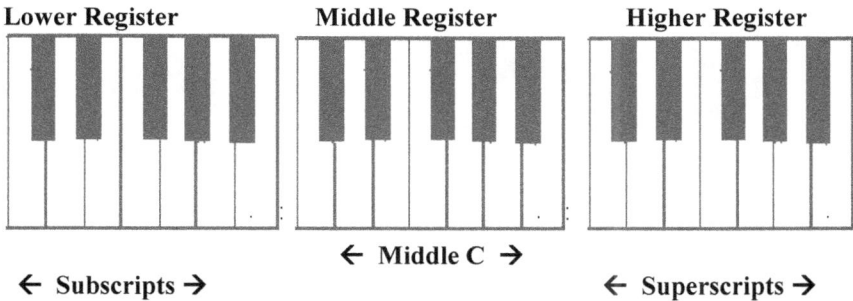

Lower Register   **Middle Register**   **Higher Register**

← Middle C →

← Subscripts →   ← Superscripts →

BRIEF INSTRUCTIONS

1. Cut out the squares and stick them on to the black and white keys.

2. Hit the notes asked for in the tonic sol-fa tunes, trying to hear each melody as a whole and keeping a steady beat.

Key to Tonic Sol-fa Notes
D = doh
R = ray
M = me
F = fah
S = soh
L = lah
T = te

WHITE KEYS: STICK-ON LABELS
FOR YOUR KEYBOARD

LOWER REGISTER	Doh_1	Ray_1	Me_1	Fah_1	Soh_1	Lah_1	Te_1
MIDDLE REGISTER	Doh	Ray	Me	Fah	Soh	Lah	Te
HIGHER REGISTER	Doh^1	Ray^1	Me^1	Fah^1	Soh^1	Lah^1	Te^1

BLACK KEYS: STICK-ON LABELS
FOR YOUR KEYBOARD

LOWER REGISTER	De_1	Maw_1	Fe_1	Law_1	Taw_1
MIDDLE REGISTER	De	Maw	Fe	Law	Taw
HIGHER REGISTER	De^1	Maw^1	Fe^1	Law^1	Taw^1

APPENDIX

HOW TO IMPROVE YOUR SINGING

In singing these songs there are seven main aspects of singing to check out and practice towards perfection. (There are also several more subtle, complex and minor aspects which only a real-life music teacher could explain. Each aspect of singing calls for separate exercises as well as putting all six together.

1. Voice Quality
Largely a given, quality can be developed by practice, healthy diet and deep breathing.

2. Diction
Concentrate on sharp clear pronunciation to achieve understanding on the part of the listener. Aim for sounds that most people with standard English, not accents, will understand.

3. Projection
Throw out the voice until all the audience can hear it. Every word must always reach the listener.

4. Phrasing
A phrase is a group of words and notes that are grouped together. Watch how the sounds and words hang together and change the combinations until it sounds right to you in your opinion. What is right for one singer may not be right for another.

5. Feeling
Try to imagine how the sender of the message would feel and think. Develop a dramatic empathy, a oneness with the message of the song so that it comes over as genuine.

6. Rhythm
Keep an even beat or a creative subtly uneven one. Tap your foot on the ground or follow a drummer, or hand claps (see also the section on timing).

7. True Notes
Make sure that the note you play is the right one. Listen to a self-tape and compare your notes with those sung by a friend or played on a keyboard or other instrument. Sometimes it helps to close your eyes and listen well.

8. Find a Teacher
If you can, find a good singing teacher with top credentials or at least get a musical friend to critique you.

THE END

www.ingramcontent.com/pod-product-compliance
Lightning Source LLC
Chambersburg PA
CBHW070537030426
42337CB00016B/2238